Copyright © 2016 Scott Fishman
All Rights Reserved
ISBN: 9781520433769

Dedicated to David Fishman, without whom I would not have this innate power of influence. Watching you gave me the foundation for this exciting and evolving career. Thank you Dad.

The 30 Minute Sales Coach Presents...

Sell Smarter

Seven Simple Strategies for Sales Success

by Scott Fishman

"I can't make a sale to save my life."

We've all heard it before. Even worse, we've all said it before. If it came down to it and you really would die without a sale, you'd find a way to sell.

Standard victim mentality has us immediately blaming the leads, the product, favoritism, nepotism, weather, holidays, etc... It's OK. Like I said, we've all been there.

I am here to give you the secrets to getting past these speed bumps. The truth is, no matter how hard we want to project the fault on external forces, odds are the key to finding sales success lies within you.

I have been there many times in my career. Driving myself nuts trying to figure out why others are finding success while I am getting shot down left and right.

By the same token, I have also been part of the opposite conversation countless times. Fielding calls and emails from peers and leaders asking what I am doing to find success where others are hitting brick walls.

In over two decades in sales, I've learned to recognize when these slumps and streaks are starting in both myself and those around me. Although the problem is not always the same, the root of the problem can be one of many issues that can plague even the best salespeople.

In the pages that follow, we will identify many of these issues and work out solutions to get past them.

Get out of your own way.

From the day I started leading and coaching new salespeople, I repeated this mantra: We are our own worst enemies in so many respects. If we just get past the hurdles we create for ourselves, success is right there.

Whether we are temporarily insane due to some emotional event, temporary stress, bad sales call, or we rat hole our selves with metrics and all the reasons we cannot succeed, we are 90% of the problem.

It's so easy to see from the outside looking in, but inside that bubble, these obstacles become very real to us. Molehills become mountains. Speed bumps become roadblocks. We create the insurmountable from the minuscule.

Just as any salesperson worth their weight will foreshadow their entire sales process, I believe that making a new salesperson conscious of these common issues up front will make them more cognizant of them when they do occur and they will recognize them either on their own or when they are pointed out by a peer, leader or coach.

In this book, we will examine common obstacles new salespeople put in front of themselves and decode them. We will find ways to not only get around these "roadblocks" but to truly blast right through them.

My goal is to have you recognize these behaviors and emotions in your own day to day and work to squash them. We truly are our own worst enemy at times. Remove that adversary and watch the road to success open up.

It's time to get out of your own way and succeed in sales.

CHAPTER ONE
Shut Up & Listen

Shut the hell up and listen.

As salespeople, we are always on stage. Every sales presentation is a performance. Proper preparation means we take time to research our product and also our prospect before we even think of presenting.

The problem is, we often neglect the latter. We overload with product knowledge and skimp on researching our client's needs.

As a result sometimes we come in over-prepared. These cases usually come in when we are at our weakest. I mean, who has time to spend hours over-preparing for a presentation when we are running from appointment to appointment closing sales left and right? Riding a hot streak allows you to fly fast and loose, winning on momentum alone!

It's often when we are slumping that we put so much pressure on ourselves and grip the bat way too tight, trying to make sure we have all bases covered. We forget that the transaction is really just between two humans and over-think it all.

Over-prepping leads to quite a few pitfalls, one of which is such a simple speed bump to get past, yet we fall prey to it over and over. We simply stop listening.

I have seen salespeople from the bottom of production reports to the top fall prey to this. We are the experts after all, so we know what is best for the customer, so we tell them what is best. We put on our little performance and show much we know. The problem is, we know everything there is to know about what we are selling and nothing about who we are selling to.

So if our problem is not truly knowing the client, what is the solution? The answer is pretty darn easy in theory, but surprisingly sometimes very difficult in practice. We just need to shut our mouths and open our ears!

"Are you really listening... or just waiting for your turn to talk?" – Robert Montgomery

I have used this line so many times in coaching folks, that at one point, I found myself searching for another quote that embodied the same sentiment in a less sarcastic tone.

"The quieter you become, the more you can hear." – Ram Dass

This one not only does the trick, but makes me sound even wiser than I already am.

If you've ever taken a Dale Carnegie course or read one of his books, you know as humans, we have a fondness for talking about ourselves. This is a universal archetype that is rarely deviated from.

Ever go to a family function and get chatted up by a distant Aunt or Uncle that you'd never met and left feeling that you really liked that person? Did you suddenly realize that you actually knew very little about them, but they sure asked a lot of questions about you? The truth is, you fell in like with them because of how they made you feel. You loved telling them all about your crazy summer adventures, sporting events or future plans. I am sure they lived vicariously through you as well, but chances are, you had more fun than they did.

Police and Con Artists alike use this type of social engineering all the time. They get you talking about yourself, and ask you questions leading down a very comfortable path. Before you know it, you are letting out some juicy bit of info that you'd have been better suited keeping to yourself. The next step is changing your passwords or calling an attorney!

We've established that people love

talking about themselves, and given the chance will tattle on themselves. Let's use this to our advantage. Think about your last few sales calls. Who did the majority of the talking? If you didn't make the sale, chances are it was you! If so, you're doing it wrong. It's time to shut the fuck up and listen. I mean really listen.

We know that our clients are human. This means it's a pretty sure shot that they will enjoy talking about themselves. Get them talking.

If you're selling to an individual, ask them general questions that you can drill down further into. For instance, if I were selling windows, I might start with "This is a great house you have here. Are you the original owner?" A question like this sometimes gets a quick one word "yes" or "no", but will often open up a whole new line of questioning that can eventually lead into us talking about the windows. We can obtain a ton of info without going right in for the kill and discussing our product such as how old the home is, has it been renovated, how long they plan to stay in the home, budget tolerances, heating/cooling costs, style preferences, etc... All of this info can be found before we offer up any info about our product.

Now our sales pitch can be molded on the fly to help address their specific needs without sounding like a canned presentation.

What sounds better?

Holding up a sample window: "Our patented three-ply glass coating has special polymers that will dramatically reduce your heating and cooling costs each year."

or

Handing them the sample window: "You mentioned this place was a bitch to keep cool in the summer. Check this out. Our windows have this space age coating, kind of like your iPhone screen. It keeps hot on the hot side and cold on the cold side. Feel how cool this stays? This will get that AC bill down for sure."

Not only are you offering them a benefit vs. a feature, but you are also relating it directly to them based on a concern you uncovered while listening to them early on. You are able to touch the emotional nerve vs. just giving them facts. People buy on emotion. They justify with logic.

Had you just walked in and started out with "Tell me why you want new windows", the answer is more often than not that the old ones are just old, or they are ugly and don't match. By having the initial fact finding conversation casually, people will tell you the real reason they want to buy and not just the answer they think you are looking for.

Note the word casual above. Nothing reeks of evidence collection more than a guy with a clipboard. Captain Clipboard will always put people on edge. Taking notes is fine, but do it casually. If I am the window guy, I have a small notepad that I keep in my pocket and take notes sparingly so I am armed with the proper ammo later. Remember, our goal is to get them talking, not to have a game of verbal Ping-Pong ensue.

What happens when you get that client who is just such a defensive nerd that he/she won't give up any info? We've all had these customers. They play their cards so close to the vest in fear that they will give you that one nugget of info that allows you to go for the jugular and leave them penniless wearing nothing but an old barrel.

First off, you are smart enough to buy this book and I assume good enough to have closed at least one sale before, so presumably you are charismatic enough to hold a conversation with another human with some level of skill. If this is the case, I pry open the closed mouth client by calling attention to the elephant in the room. "Jon... it is clear to me that you have some apprehension here. I want to assure you that my only goal here is to help you. Any questions I ask are really meant to move us down the path of determining if we are a right fit for each other. This isn't an 'anything you say can and will be used against you' situation. My aim is to leave you in a better position than I found you."

I'm not gonna lie, this one is not totally foolproof, but the small amount of people you alienate with a statement like this, would either not have done business with you anyway, or would have taken up five client's worth of time to make one sale. The folks who do get it will slowly loosen up. Just ask them questions that are pertinent and pull at threads. Ask these folks too many questions about that dog barking in the background or what breakfast cereal they like will shut them right back down.

With this chapter being all about shutting our face holes, there is one age-old sales maxim that I feel the need to bring up before we move on. "The first one to speak loses" has been thrown around for years. When it comes to a negotiation, it definitely holds water. When it comes to closing a deal, it works too… conditionally. You have to know your client though. Since this technique is well known, clients will often do it right back to you causing a very uncomfortable phone silence or staring contest.

Being prepared for this is important. Again, I like to de-fuse the silence with some humor.

"Louis, now is the time where you are supposed to ask me how we get everything started. This is no time to be shy. Let me grab that paperwork and I will walk you through the next steps..."

Or, you can just be matter of fact.

"It sounds like you don't have any more questions. Did you want to pay by check or take advantage of our financing options?"

I'm guessing that 75% of the time these statements will bring out further objections, which get you closer to a close. If you already earned the close though, they might just be the icebreaker needed to get them to sign on the dotted line.

Homework

If it's not clear to you yet that this chapter is all about listening, you probably aren't listening to the words I am typing. Ever do that? Read page after page of a book, but not pay attention at all then have to go back and re-read it all over again? Happens to me all the time. Don't do it with my books though. Get your money's worth!

Okay, back to the challenge. This challenge will be more fun if you enjoy an occasional adult beverage, but possible without one as well. I want you to go sit at a bar, alone. Your job is to extract as much info out of the bartender as you can without he/she learning too much about you. This will be hard since good bartenders do the exact opposite to you.

The challenge is to win by 7. Track it with a little tick sheet or something similarly rudimentary so you don't look like a cub reporter taking notes. If you get seven pieces of info before they get any, you win. If they ask your name or where you're from, that counts, so they score one and you must reach 8. Keep going until your score exceeds theirs by seven. At some point they will probably think you are hitting on them. Who knows, it could even end up in a date (I keep saying that sales is like dating anyway).

Complete this challenge, and it will be that much easier next time you start a conversation with a prospect when you have a common interest between you.

CHAPTER TWO
Follow Your Noes

Follow your "Noes"

No, sucks. We offer to buy a girl a drink and they say "no thanks" and our confidence is kicked in the nuts. Even worse, we walk back over to our buddies and they aren't exactly offering a shoulder to cry on. I liken sales to dating all the time. I always say that my greatest sale was convincing my wife to sign on the dotted line of that marriage license, knowing all of the weirdness and humanity that came with me.

If you are a man in sales, you no doubt lived through this in your youth and maybe still do. If you are a woman in sales, you either lived through this at some point or the exact opposite. I bet when you started in sales, you started to empathize with those poor saps offering to buy you a Cosmo in exchange for some polite conversation.

It's no wonder that we have this unfounded fear of hearing no. Look at your average conversion. Ratios will differ depending on your field, but I think it is safe to say that a 10-20% conversion from lead to sale is solid. This means that out of 100 people you speak to, minimum, 80 are not "yeses". Thankfully, these aren't all telling you no. A good portion won't qualify in some way shape or form to use or buy the product. We can safely put that at 50% of the noes. This leaves us with 40-45 prospects telling us, or our prospectors to take a hike. It's real. And it can be real disheartening at times.

It's a numbers game. Knowing that such a large portion of our leads will be "noes" right off the bat is both a blessing and a curse. What if the "yeses" are the

LAST ten to twenty people we talk to? Even worse in the pessimist's eyes, what if the first ten people are "yeses". Will you assume the next ninety will be telling you where to shove your product? Numbers don't lie right? Why even get out of bed if we know we are going to just hear "no" all day?

In reality, it is usually, somewhere right in the middle. Our yeses will be sprinkled amongst the noes. This is why we have to learn to recognize hot and cold streaks early.

If you've ever gambled or played a competitive sport (are there non-competitive sports?), you've experienced being in the zone. You win seemingly twenty hands of Blackjack in a row, doubling down and still winning. What do you do when you lose three in a row? Do you press? Or do you recognize that the streak may be over and get up from the table with a pile of newfound chips?

You're on the basketball court and you are draining buckets like Cousin Terio left and right. Nothing is missing. So you start launching threes from just over half court. You quickly lay a few bricks. Chances are, the coach is about to pull you and give you a rest. You are starting to get in your own way!

The same thing happens to us as salespeople. We hear no on our first 7 or 8 prospects. We don't even get to present our product. It's just stonewall city and the clients just don't want to listen to what we have to say. What do we do? The very next person we talk to is already prejudged to be no #9 of the day. We just know that they are going to be an asshole. It's definitely them, how could it be us, right?

At this point, I want you to take a breather. If it's only 10 or 11 am, go to lunch or the gym. Go take a walk around Best Buy and play with video games (this always worked for me). It doesn't matter what you do; just do something. You are cancerous to your own sale at this point. Call it a morning. Come back late afternoon and start A NEW DAY. This is very important. If you cannot shake off the crap from the morning, call it a day. Same thing if it's after 1pm and you hit the dry spell. Stop putting good money after bad. You won't win.

Remember, it is a numbers game. But people also buy on emotion and energy. We've all had that day where we just knew the next prospect was signing on the dotted line. They were no match for us and they wanted the product and could afford the product. We are in the zone! Here's where you must resist the urge to celebrate your good day. Remember, a bad day is lurking around the corner, so make hay while the sun shines. Play the hot hand until you get a predetermined number of noes. Remember the guy with the hot hand in basketball. Once he hit a few bricks in a row and took some chances, coach was ready to pull him. Ride your wave until you lay those bricks.

There is a saying I like. "Don't let your highs get too high and your lows too low." Simply put, if you have a great day, don't go put money down on a Bentley and start popping Dom. You're bound to come down to earth eventually. On the flip, if you have a bad day, there is no reason to start questioning yourself or checking to see if those 10th floor windows open. You've had success in the past. You will have success again. Know it in your heart and you will find it tomorrow.

  Learn to take every no as being one step closer to the next yes. I had an old Sales Manager who, despite being a racist prick, had some good advice that I have passed on to countless proteges over the years. In this job, I had to cold call teachers out of the employee phone book. I was 23 or 24 at the time and saw myself as anything but an authority. This may as well have been cleaning septic tanks as much as I hated it. So my boss made a deal with me. If I got twenty-five noes every night, I was done. How hard could that be? Just make twenty-five calls and call it an evening. Piece of cake!!!

  The oddest thing happened to me though. I wasn't done in 25 calls. I was so focused on getting to the 25 noes, that I started getting "yeses"! It actually took me about 28-30 calls to get to 25 noes because I was actually finding success and booking appointments! That drunk fucker totally twisted me up. I was no longer worried about a no because I wanted a no.

Every time one of my reports or proteges complains that they can't get a yes, I toss this challenge. It is amazing how well it works. I've recently tossed it at seasoned salespeople with mindset issues. It works!

Something to keep in mind, which is actually the opposite of dating, is that when a prospect says no, they are not always saying no to you. They may be saying no to the company, product, or even the timing of your sale. Don't take it personally. Now, if you offer to buy a guy or a gal a drink and they flat out say no, it may be time for a stylist, or a dentist, or maybe a shower because they are saying no to you.

Something else to keep in mind is that noes and yeses are not permanent. We've all had fickle clients back out on us and leads we thought were gone forever come calling a week or two later saying "I'm ready" and leaving us scratching our heads. So don't burn that bridge.

Resist the urge to take it personal and tell a "no" where they can stick that no. Resist the urge to badmouth your competition. Let them drop the ball themselves. Not everyone is as agile as you. Some folks need to deliberate. Some need to kick the tires, put irons in the fire, mull it over, build a spreadsheet, talk to their spouse and end our call with "Well, I got your number..., I will call you.". Politely thank them for their time and set a firm follow-up. I guarantee every other schmoe they are talking to is fuming and starting to get short with them at this point (unless of course, they bought this book as well). Kill the no with kindness and a funny thing happens. You win! That same person who is blowing you off is also blowing off your less calm competition. Handle this right and increase your bottom line.

Homework

This one is easy. Find out your conversion metrics. How many sales do you need to make in a day to hit or exceed your goal (a)? How many leads does it take you to make a sale (b)?

$$(a)x(b)-(a)$$

This is the number of noes you need to hear in a day to hit your goal.

Number a sheet of paper and tick off every "no" you get throughout the day. Make a quick note as to why your prospect did not buy. The notes are important as we can also increase conversion by finding common objections to overcome.

This is exactly the exercise I was given and have assigned countless times. Focus on hearing "no" and the "yeses" will inevitably sneak in!

CHAPTER THREE
You've got to believe!

You've Got To Believe!

My first commission sales job was great. It was the mid-nineties and I took a job selling tax sheltered annuities to folks in the education and health care field. I started off doing well enough and really enjoyed the freedom of making my own hours and truly being in charge of my own destiny.

I was partial to placing folks into a specific product offered by one of America's largest investment firms. Returns were great on this particular fund and the name recognition afforded by its firm made this a no-brainer sale that I was able to work people into a froth to get into. I mastered that one product and made it the focus of my sale. Clients ate it up. My shtick was strong and the returns were obvious.

Then, "tragedy" struck. I found out that the product I was so keen on selling was also available in the majority of my territory directly from the investment firm. This meant that my clients could reap the benefits of my pet product while cutting out the middleman (me) and save themselves hundreds, potentially thousands in maintenance and transaction fees.

Finding this out crushed my confidence. I had spent the previous six months or so, honing the sale on this product to the point of selling myself thoroughly on it. In my eyes, there was no other product as powerful for my clients. The problem was, I started to believe that I was irrelevant. Why did they need me if they could get it cheaper elsewhere.

Looking back, I know that I was the differentiator. When they cut out the middleman, they also cut out the adviser and were left to their own devices to manage their retirement funds. I really was worth the extra cost (an extra cost mind you, that the client usually didn't even know existed), but twenty-five year old me was too naive to see that. All I saw was that I was "screwing" the client by not telling them about the direct option.

My ability to sell that product was lost, because I no longer believed it was the best for the client. I never recovered from this. Anytime I found a new fund to push, all I saw were the reasons my company was non-essential to the client in the process.

This is why I want you to find a way to believe in what you are selling. Customers can sense when you are "selling" them. They can tell when you don't care. But when you can genuinely demonstrate that you not only understand the problem you are solving for them, but also fully believe that your product will help, they will feel it and ultimately buy your product.

At the same time, one trap I want you to never fall into is lying to the customer. Telling them you use your product when you really don't is not only unethical, but it is also transparent. You will eventually be found out. Losing your integrity as a salesperson is the kiss of death.

Dogfooding

Dogfooding is a great way to get to know your product and build the familiarity with how it adds benefit to your life. Many companies encourage their employees to "eat their own dog food".

This term is said to have originated from one of two places. The first possible origin is from the original Alpo Dog Food commercials where spokesman Lorne Greene pointed out that he fed Alpo to his own dogs. The second, less appetizing origin story comes from Kal Kan Dog Food, where the president of the company was rumored to start shareholder' meetings off by chowing down on a bowl of Kal Kan.

Regardless of the back-story, a manager at Microsoft in the late nineties by the name of Paul Maritz is credited for a now famous email where he encouraged Microsoft employees to "Eat our own dogfood" and increase internal usage of Microsoft's products.

Regardless of where the term comes from, dogfooding is invaluable. Who better to sell a product than a satisfied customer? You become even more of a trusted adviser in this respect. How easy is it to get a friend to binge-watch a TV show that you love? Your enthusiasm for House of Cards or Game of Thrones is infectious and gets them excited to watch it themselves. Your seal of approval goes far! On the flip side, your seal of disapproval holds even more weight. Think about the faces we make when offered a food we can't stand. That grimace far outweighs the face we make when offered our favorite treat. People are more demonstrative about things that bring them pain.

One such story I have about lying about the product takes it to the extreme. Years ago, I was in a training class for a position in the mortgage industry. A friend of mine was in that very same class.

As part of our training, we were coached on live calls with potential prospects. My buddy was building great rapport with a potential client and due to his inexperience, he was circling around the loan products he was putting together for the client and the client was questioning it. The trainer who was working with him had him put the prospect on hold and told my buddy to say "This is the product for you. It is the one I have on my own mortgage right now". The problem was, my buddy was NOT a homeowner. He was renting and did not yet own his own home. He uncomfortably got back on the phone and to his credit, he did not use the line he was told to use. In the end, he did not earn the client's business that day, but he did earn the client's trust. We will never know how that story ends though, because there was never a follow-up as my friend handed in his resignation the next day because he did not feel comfortable with being encouraged to lie to a potential client.

If it is not possible for you to use your product yourself due to you not being the target market or any other reason, you can still find many ways to build your belief in the product. Client testimonials are a great way to see what past customers have said about the product. These customer reviews are great for helping you figure out what features offered what benefit for customers. As well as building your confidence in knowing that your product really did do the trick for folks.

Knowing all of the features and benefits of your product is key to this. You need to understand why a customer needs your product and why they should want the product as well. Uncovering their need will help you tailor your explanation of how the features will benefit them. Once the customer grasps the reason they want it, their need then becomes having the product. Our job is turning that initial need into want.

Picture your perfect customer avatar. What are the top 5 problems they are solving with your product? Each customer might have one unique reason for needing the product, but figure out the top five reasons that will bring people through the door.

Now match up one of the features of your product with each of those top five. Take careful notes. To be clear, this is not your sale. This is the outline of what you must know in order to hone your presentation.

Now, take each of those features and write a paragraph or two about the benefit they will receive from said feature. From here, your sales pitch is taking shape. To the average car buyer, the navigation package is merely a four-figure line item in an ever expanding list of features that inflate the cost of their car. When they hear the story of how one of your favorite clients got turned around on a back road in Hazzard County and was able to utilize the non-cellular dependent satellite navigation system to find their way back to the highway, and make it to their only granddaughter's graduation on time, it paints a picture.

Reaching out to past customers for testimonials like these is a great practice. Not only do you get usable material for your future sales calls, but you also show them that you do care about them after the sale. Don't forget to ask for referrals!

This is not our last discussion of features vs. benefits, as we will certainly talk about them more in this and subsequent books. Knowing the benefits will help you gain the belief in your product that you need to sell effectively.

Homework

Take a few minutes and write down your favorite TV show, movie, food, and social destination. Over the course of the next week, I want you to convince (not sell) a friend, co-worker or family member to try each of these for themselves.

Assess each conversation afterward. What types of words did you use? How did your voice sound? At what point in the conversation did you sense that you had convinced them to try it out?

If you took this assignment seriously, you chose something you already had passion for, so selling someone on trying it out is not that difficult. Take the enthusiasm, tone and words you used in this exercise and apply it to your sales presentation.

CHAPTER FOUR
Don't Be a Lyman

Make friends with them. Don't just sell them.

It's a fact that people will by from someone they like. One of the easiest ways to prove this is looking at the opposite statement for corroboration. People will rarely buy from someone they don't' like. Ever met a top salesperson that was a total dick? If so, did you observe them around their clients? I bet they were the exact opposite when in the zone. They flip the switch and become super personable when it counts. This is important. The key is, to be genuine.

Customers are already on guard. Being patronizing, pedantic, or fake is super transparent. Remember, our prospects are on high alert at first and really have no reason to trust us, so odds are they won't until we earn it. If their spider sense is already activated and we are fake to them, they will pick up on it immediately.

How do we make friends in our day-to-day lives? We find common ground. I can't tell you how many games of Jewish Geography I took part in growing up, where we figured out who we knew in common 'Six Degrees of Kevin Bacon' style. Whether it's a common friend or a shared interest, it is easy to make friends when we relate to the person we are interacting with in some way.

One way to put them at ease is to humanize yourself. Put them on equal ground. When we approach a strange dog, we offer them a limp hand to show them we mean no harm. We should be doing the same with our customers. One way I do this with my clients (which is sadly all too real) is apologizing up front for a cough or losing my voice due to allergies kicking in. A good 80% of my prospects acknowledge that they too feel my pain. Whoah! Just like that, we are brothers in arms. A few tasteful self-deprecating jokes tossed in, along with a humble brag or two "Yeah, they make the old guys like me work from home so the young kids don't know what kind of pricing we get for our clients." and we're in. Answer their questions properly, show them what they want and close.

A topic to avoid starting a conversation with is weather. It's a straight up tee-ball conversation and odds are, your competition is using it as well. It's not a topic to avoid altogether, since it is top of mind, but if I hear you say, "How's the weather up there?" on a phone call, you will instantly lose 10 charisma points.

One trap that is super important to avoid is being too nice. That guy who is a dick at the office and suave with his clients has this mastered. He/She earns their customers respect and trust through knowledge and mastery while earning their like by humanizing themselves and entertaining the prospect. He/She displays that they will confidently go to war for their clients… and win.

If we are too nice and accommodating we turn ourselves into a Lyman; Lyman is a guy I worked with years ago. He was handsome, funny, a great dancer and kind beyond belief. Lyman's achilles heel is that folks liked him a ton, but had no respect for him. Prospects had no issue saying no to Lyman. And he had no problem saying "OK" to their no. He hadn't earned the right to be the master and expert.

We all work for our clients, but Lyman turned himself into their employee. Along these same lines, Lyman had trouble keeping clients because they were not afraid to call him after they initially said yes and back out of a deal. They were right not to be afraid, because he really did just say "OK" to them when they called him back with the lamest of excuses. He never fought back and poked holes in their flawed logic. He just took it. If we have done our job correctly, the clients should have some fear of calling us to back out because they know we will merely remind them off all the reasons they said yes to begin with. Our job is to sell them and re-sell them. If we let them back out after saying yes, remind them of what life is like without your product. Don't be a Lyman.

Homework

You get to watch TV for homework! Watch an episode or two from an earlier season, then a later season of Entourage. If you haven't ever watched the show, I recommend it. For about $15, you can have HBO on demand for a month and a copy of this book. What a great investment in your career!

In the earlier season, look at the difference between how Ari and Lloyd are perceived by their clients. Ari's clients have absolute faith that he is going to bust down doors and negotiate on their behalf to a serious win. Ari also burns many bridges in doing his job. This scorched earth mentality can be very detrimental.

Lloyd on the other hand gets pushed around and is not taken seriously by his clients or his business associates. Both often go over his head and call Ari. They do not trust he can get the job done.

As the show progresses and the characters evolve, Ari begins to grow a heart. People start to see the good in him and he sacrifices a bit of his bullishness to show some vulnerability that ultimately pays dividends.

On the opposite end of the spectrum, Lloyd grows some more balls. He learns when and how to take control of the situation and his clients. This gives him more of an aura of invincibility which pays off when he shows his clients what he is capable of and grows.

You need to learn when to be an Ari and when to be a Lloyd. And never, under any circumstances, be a Lyman.

CHAPTER FIVE
Set Goal-Di-Locks

Don't aim too low or too high. Aim just right.

Goals are important. Without intelligent goal setting, we have nothing to aim for and no direction. As salespeople, the vast majority of us are the masters or mistresses of our own domain. We dictate how well we do and how hard we push. We may have a manager or team lead, but for the most part, we are our own boss. Improperly setting goals is a major way that we sabotage our business.

The first danger in goal setting is setting our goals too high. Everyone wants to succeed, and face it, if we didn't want to make more money, we'd find an easier salary job to settle into. In this respect it is all too easy to sit down at the beginning of a month, quarter or year and set an outrageous goal to shoot for. These goals are great because they give us something to shoot for that is beyond our normal reach. You must build your sales muscle to get there.

Much like lifting weights though, very few of us can walk into a gym, say "I'm going to bench press 300 pounds", lie down on the bench and toss it up. You have to first test your own tolerance for what you can lift and gradually build up to heavier weights. If you set proper incremental goals, you can work up to that 300lb lift in time.

Goal setting for sales is very much the same. You have to first get your baseline and see what you can achieve on a daily/weekly/monthly and extrapolate goals from there. Ratchet these up accordingly and you will eventually get to levels you never believed you could achieve.

Try to bench press 300lbs when you have never lifted seriously before, and you will more than likely get hurt; both physically and your pride. In the same vein, set your sales goals too high and you will not only hurt your pride, but it creates a losing mindset. In our business, mindset plays such a huge role. It can make or break you. We need wins, even small ones, along the way to keep the right mindset. Don't get me wrong, missing a goal here and there doesn't make you a loser, but at the same time, purposely setting goals we know we will miss by a landslide does no good.

Setting goals that we are sure to miss does something else to our mindset. We start to rationalize missing goals. Once it becomes "OK" to not hit a goal because "I knew it wasn't attainable, I just did it to stretch myself", it starts to creep in that any goal we set is not firm. When we start to see goals as suggestions, mediocrity enters our life.

On the other end, setting goals that are too easy gives us a lot of little wins, but we end up not growing. Think of the weightlifter that never challenges himself or the chubby guy who gets on the treadmill and goes the same time/distance/speed every day (yeah... I am looking in the mirror). They may lose weight, but progress will be much slower than if they challenge themselves.

When our goals are too attainable, it becomes all too easy to start strong and taper off. We allow ourselves to slack knowing that we are so close to the goal that we can coast. Have you ever had that month where on the 20th, you are pacing to exceed a goal then inexplicably on the 30th, you are scrambling to find more business to make it to the goal? You are not alone, this happens all the time. It occurs because we let it. Our goal was small enough that we fool ourselves into thinking we don't have to try.

Similarly, setting goals too low stunts are growth. We grow complacent with hitting the easy goal and the false positive we get from it. Once this occurs, we begin to rationalize our business and build our own glass ceiling. Our mindset then has us fooled into thinking we are capped at this attainable goal and we never stretch.

You might be thinking, "Are you crazy Scott?" We can't set goals too high and we can't set them too low. How do we find that Goldilocks level?

Much like that weightlifter, we have to find out what we are capable of at a baseline first. Once you have a baseline, you can ratchet it up to achieve growth. Pull your numbers for the last quarter. What did you do per day/week/month? It's safe to say that since you have done it, it's possible.

Now figure out what you want your increase to be? What is possible? What did the top producer in the company do? It is also safe to assume that this is also possible. Are you as experienced as they are? Do they possess something you don't? This is what I mean by not reaching TOO high. If someone has already done it, it is possible. If they can do it, so can you. If you feel that this goal is the equivalent of that 300lb bench press, set your initial goal right in between what you did and what the top producer did and increase accordingly as you hit milestones along the way.

What if you are brand new at the company and have no metrics to go on? Again, look at what other folks have produced most recently. Do you feel that you have what it takes to be #1 out of the gate? If so, aim for the top. If not, take the top ten producers and find where the cliff is. Where is there a large jump in #s? If the number 6 performer far out-produces 7-10, set your sights on beating #6. Look at the entire top ten in this way. If the cliff is between #3 and #4, make #3 your rabbit and chase them.

Now... What if you are in the enviable position of being the top performer already? Remember, everyone below you is gunning for you, so you won't stay number one for long if you stay stat quo. You must set goals that will help you grow your business and income. This is a point where I like to have fun with goals. Chances are, if you are at the top already, you are making a fine living for yourself. Set a goal that allows you to reward yourself. What will this increase in sales for the month, quarter or year allow you to do that might be outside of your normal spending zone? Down payment on a vacation home? Serious upgrade in the automotive department? Maybe the big daddy Rolex? Money can't buy happiness, but it sure can buy some cool stuff. And cool stuff can seriously alter your mindset to the positive, which can then increase your bottom line and earn you even more money.

Once you set your realistic goals, it is time to break them down. Take your quarterly goal and break it down to monthly goals. Evaluate this. Is it a stretch, yet attainable? Is it an increase over what you have been doing? If so, skip weekly goals and go directly to daily. This is hugely important because every month has different amounts of business days and holidays. Be sure to take into account any planned vacation time (if you are not taking any vacation time, please start doing do immediately). Divide your monthly goal by actual business days. Is this daily number a stretch, yet attainable? Good!

We are almost there.

Pull out your calendar and figure out where you need to be each Friday to hit your goal. Now is where we will mind-fuck ourselves a bit. Take ALL of your Friday goals and multiply them by 1.1. "Wait, you told us to keep our goals attainable and not overreach. This is counter intuitive." I hear you. But we <u>are</u> out to grow our business remember? I've been a little soft on you and chances are, you played it a little safe so far. What is a ten percent increase really? If you normally make two sales a day, that's ten a week. Increasing that by ten percent is ONE MORE SALE. That extra sale is gravy. Remember, we are NOT increasing your monthly or quarterly goals one iota. With thirteen weeks in the quarter, if you hit that extra one sale every other week you are ensured not to be scrambling at the last minute. In fact, you'd only have to make four sales in that last week to hit your goal. If you were able to hit the extra ten percent EVERY week, you'll blast through your goal a full week early.

This is a numbers game. It is important to see things not only as a marathon, but also a series of small sprints that make up the race. When you break down your quarter, know that you will have strong days/weeks/months and weak ones to boot. Proper goal setting will allow you to earn the living you desire without the stress of scrambling to hit the goal. As an added benefit, not having that last minute stress means you don't have to sound desperate in the end. Clients smell fear and when you are pressuring them after the 25th of a month, they know they have the upper hand as you are trying to hit your goal.

Homework

Sit down and map out your yearly, quarterly, monthly, weekly and daily goals. Once you have them clearly laid out, find an accountability partner who you can do scheduled check-ins with. Put these check-ins in your calendar and do not miss them.

Your partner is merely there to check on you. They do not have to coach you if they/you do not want. Hit a goal? Celebrate with a high-five and keep running to stay ahead of pace for the next milestone. Miss a goal? Question the why, but don't dwell on it. Make adjustments to subsequent goals and move on. Remember, you are focusing on these mile markers toward your ultimate destination.

CHAPTER SIX
No Perfect Time

There is no perfect time

One other way we get in our own way is waiting for the perfect time to call a client and even worse, the perfect time to close.

No one wants to look like they are just sitting by the phone waiting for your call. How often do you call on a prospect that is just "hanging out"? They want to sound busy. Think about all the times you catch someone who is on a conference call, in a meeting or "just walking into a meeting". Let's just agree to something here. One, if you are ON a conference call, you aren't putting it on hold to take a random sales call. Two, if you are in a meeting, you aren't calling time-out to take a call on your cell. And three, look at your watch the next time you say you are walking into a meeting. We know meetings don't start promptly at 11:18 am these days.

With that little rant out of the way, never wait around for the perfect time to call. Does the following sound familiar?

We don't want to call before 9am because they are in traffic.

We don't want to call between nine and ten because they are just starting their day.

We call around ten-thirty and they are engrossed in whatever they started doing at 9:30. They want a call at lunch.

We call during lunch and get voice mail.

We don't want to call right after lunch because we know they will be busy with returning their calls and emails from lunch and the morning.

So we wait until two-ish in the afternoon to call. By this time, we are lethargic and frustrated with "chasing them" even though WE created the chase and procrastinations. They pick up and when they sound busy, we offer the objection of calling after five.

We call at 5:15 as promised while they are in the car and get voice mail because they got stuck in the office. So we decide to call back tomorrow, rinse, repeat.

What you must do instead is call first thing. If they are busy, they will tell you. Book a solid time for a follow up. If you get them to commit to a time, you can hold them accountable when they miss it and they will respect you. They also won't repeat the missing of appointments. You will gain that valuable meeting and more than likely a new client, all because you did not give yourself the excuse.

To me, closing a sale is a lot like dating. Along those same lines, the first close is like the first kiss. There are few things more awkward than that first date where you have the jitters all night. She's wondering if you are going to make a move, you're trying to figure out all night how to be smooth and say the right thing at the right time with the right light and lean in for that movie kiss. In reality what happens is either an awkward hug/handshake/peck, a completely out of context mauling or in many cases the drinks kind of "make it happen" and you really don't have rhyme or reason.

Imagine, if when you picked her up you said "Here's how I'd like to see the night go. I am going to take you to a nice dinner and we'll finish off a nice bottle of Pinot. Then we'll hit that new Rom Com and I'll probably try to hold your hand a little. I might even do the yawn that turns into an arm around the shoulders. After the movie, maybe we'll grab a nightcap and I will walk you to your door. Provided I haven't made an ass of myself, I will take that moment to steal my first kiss with you."

Now if she had an objection to that foreshadow of the evening, she might just let you know right away. If she doesn't, it is safe to assume that things will progress as stated unless otherwise interrupted with texts from a sick friend or you getting slapped for saying something inappropriate. At the end of the night, you will be feeling pretty confident as you walk her to the door. There might even be an Air Supply song playing in your head as the lighting is indeed perfect and you get that kiss just like in the movie you saw earlier.

Closing is just like that kiss! If you take the time to foreshadow how your sales presentation will go, the client cannot be or even act surprised when you walk over to them with Air Supply playing in your head and lean in for that open mouthed close. How can they? You mapped out exactly what you were going to do up front. They knew that you were going to present your product or service to them and that they would have ample time to ask questions as you deftly answered them and handled all objections before going in for the kill. If they had an objection, they had every opportunity to stop you beforehand. You are home free. All you need to do is ask for the business!

Of course, I am over simplifying things a bit. Simply foreshadowing the date is not going to turn you into instant Clooney. I will tell you though that going in blind, tentative and sweaty-pitted like you have in the past is a one-way trip to handshake city.

Likewise, you still have work to do between the start of your sales call and the first close, but you will be infinitely more confident as you go through the steps of your sale. That first close is also, not a guaranteed panty dropper, but at that point, your objections turn into buying signs in disguise. Handle an objection, close again. At this point, if they are not interested, they will find a way to shut you down. If they don't, repeat the process until you have exhausted their objections and they are ready to sign on the line.

Remember, just like she said yes to that date, the prospect is there for a reason. They are interested in buying your product. They wouldn't have taken the meeting otherwise. This means they enter the meeting leaning toward "yes". How we handle ourselves and the presentation can either get them leaning further that way or push them in the other direction. Knowing that they start off on our side, that proper foreshadow can set the tone. Get them further on our side of the Prime Meridian and any stumbles on our end won't push them back over the line.

Homework

Start utilizing this in your daily life outside of work. Find at least three other avenues in your life where a powerful foreshadow can sway things in our favor. Put that foreshadowing to good use.

I will share two ways my wife does this to me:

1. On Friday evening, she lays out her rough plans for her/us for the weekend. She is laying it all out there in case I have any objections up front. If I do, we adjust accordingly. If not, it is assumed the plan is OK.

2. If she wants to make a large purchase, she uses the "start high" method. "I saw this couch I wanted to buy, but it was way too expensive. $10,000 for a couch isn't something I can justify." She just leaves this out there to float in space. It's a seemingly innocuous statement right? She's setting a subconscious baseline for me. A week or

so later, I am primed for the setup when she says, "I am super excited. I found a couch similar to that $10,000 one and this one is only $4,000!" She has put that still expensive $4,000 couch on sale without it even being on sale.

I hope husbands and wives alike can both benefit from #2.

CHAPTER SEVEN
Don't Forget To Close

Don't forget to close

Would you ever consider working a full week then tell your boss to just keep the paycheck? Of course you wouldn't. Occasionally, as salespeople, we do just this. We prospect, we set appointments, we pitch, and then we set a follow-up, all without closing. Just like working that forty-hour week, going through the entire sales process without actually asking for the business is one of the dumbest things we do to get in our own way as sales folks, yet we do it every day.

Not closing comes from a few places. All of which can be addressed and tweaked in your game.

One such place not closing comes from is not recognizing when the client is ready. This can be a tough one. Very rarely does the prospect ask us "So... what's the next step from here?".

We must learn to recognize buying signs, both subtle and otherwise. If it's in person and you are pitching to more than one person, one such cue is when one client looks at the other and gives the head tilt and eyebrow as if to say "What do you think?". At this point, that non-verbal can either mean one of them is on board, both is on board or the slightly worse, neither on board. At the end of the day, it really doesn't matter, because a trial close here flushes that all out. If one is on board, you now have a sales assistant and someone to bounce things off at the other. If the trial close reveals that both are on board, you merely have to follow up with a major call to action "Sounds like everything is in order, let me fill you in on the process from here and we'll get everything rolling." If none of them are on board, the trial close offers you the opportunity to handle their objections. Responding relevantly and closing again will push you one step closer to having that aforementioned sales assistant.

When selling over the phone, one great buying sign to me is the first question that does not involve price. I like to get the price objection out of the way early by letting them know I will work with them and ensure they get the best pricing available. Everyone wants to know price because it is always a concern. I like when they ask me other questions like "What's the turn time?" or "Would we be able to tweak it like this?" At this point it's easy to toss a close out there with a call to action to get any final objections out. "We certainly could alter the payment plan to your needs. Let's go ahead and get everything started and if you change your mind on the payment terms tomorrow, we can make that switch at your request on the fly without skipping a beat." This second part will take away the objection of "OK, I will think about which way to go tonight and call you tomorrow." They've told us they want to work with us, that final piece is all that needs to be ironed out and it is the tiniest of speed bumps. No roadblocks in sight.

Of course, these are just a few generic ways to recognize that the window to closing is open. I cannot give definitive buying signs for all products, industries and situations. It's up to you to reflect back on your past sales calls to see where exactly those magic moments occurred. Hindsight is 20/20 here. It's also so much easier to recognize when it is time to close when you are not the salesperson. As a leader of sales teams, I learned to recognize the simplest non-verbal cues even without hearing both sides of the call. I could be caught waving my arms multiple times a day mouthing "CLOSE!" to my proteges even without knowing what the client on the other end of the phone was saying. You can feel the ebb and flow of the sales call just from the rhythm of the conversation.

Get me on the phone with my own clients however, and I sometimes miss simple buying signs while trying to dazzle the client with my knowledge and advice. Sometimes these things are not so visible when you are in the bubble.

I am beginning to think I may have hung with the wrong crowd as a younger man, because I have yet another quote given to me by a co-worker years ago about not knowing when to close. "You've got her lying there naked in the bed waiting and you're wasting time blowing out candles dummy." Yeah... crass, but true. Once the client is ready to buy, we can easily talk them right out of the sale.

Continue to talk when the client is ready to go, and we run the risk of feeding them objections or giving them reason to think. Every feature/benefit we give at that point has them wondering if this is really what they want or if company x down the road can do that thing better. Buyer's remorse sets in regardless. The more we bullshit with them without moving the sale forward, the higher the chances of that remorse hitting before they even buy!

Learn to recognize buying signs and capitalize. Learning when to close is something that comes with time, but when you figure out these sweet spots, your job gets that much easier. Pay attention and learn! Don't worry about the candles. If she wants them blown out, she'll let you know.

Homework

Practice makes perfect. If we find ourselves avoiding or "forgetting" the close, we must get more comfortable doing so.

Your homework is to close on every call/meeting for a week. Do not leave the room or end a call without closing in some way shape or form. Do not take no for an answer. Do not take the second no for an answer. The third no is discretionary. Do you feel you can convert the prospect? Set a follow up or close again. Is this a dead end? The third no earns you your exit.

Some of you hotshots out there are probably saying "I already do this, why wouldn't I close on every sales call?" I guarantee this is not the case. You are definitely prejudging some prospects and not seeing the benefit yourself, so you are letting the client (and yourself) off easy. EVERY SINGLE presentation this week gets closed.

Not seeing the benefit? Find one. The prospect took the meeting for a reason. State your benefit and close. Is the client trying to end the conversation abruptly? CLOSE! Make them give you an objection. If they are shooting you down, you didn't earn the close to begin with. That objection will take the conversation in the right direction.

Play your cards right this week and a few things will happen. First, you will make a couple of sales you didn't expect because you merely asked for the business. How's that for a confidence boost? Second, you will grow more and more comfortable with closing and responding to objections, which in turn will earn you more sales. Lastly, by finding success where you saw "noes" before, you will turbo charge your business and increase your conversion rate.

CHAPTER EIGHT
Final Thoughts

Final Thoughts

"Those who can't do, teach."

We've all heard it before. Shit, I've said it on more than one occasion. This statement was embodied for a generation by Tom Cruise's professor in the movie Cocktail. I've come across sales coaches that couldn't hold my jock on the sales floor and probably gave them less respect than they deserved just for trying to do their job.

Don't get it twisted, I didn't write this book in penance for disrespecting some poor sap in the past though. I wrote this book to help you… and to help me. I am a player-coach in the truest sense of the word, on the field day in and day out overcoming objections with the best and worst of you. We're in the foxhole together, working to keep my own mindset in check as I navigate waters both rough and smooth.

Another reason I was compelled to write this book is in direct response to some of the "Sales Tips" I have seen recently. I have seen so many "Mini-Wolves of Wall Street" lately sharing their successes. In my eyes, we don't have to channel high-pressure salesman from the big screen to excel in our field. It's not about pounding Red Bull and chest-bumping after we "bag a sale". Do your job right, and everybody wins.

Sales is in my blood. I cannot escape it. By harnessing it and paying it forward, I can make a difference. If I can earn each of you an extra sale, if I can get you past an objection, if I can save you from stressing out, I will consider this effort a success.

Take the lessons in this book, use them and share them. It's time to get out of your own way and find success.

CHAPTER NINE
About The Author

About The Author

Husband and father first, Scott lives in Bloomfield Hills, Michigan with his amazingly supportive wife, Beth and his two dogs, Louis and Coco.

To this day, Scott is still active in his sales career at one of the country's largest mortgage lenders. After nearly two decades in that industry, he is convinced he will be doing it forever. Over the years, he has been able to lead, coach, grow and mentor an entire generation of salespeople.

In his spare time, Scott and his pal Jon co-host The Seven Minute Sales Minute podcast which has a rapidly growing audience.

CHAPTER TEN
Endnotes

Thank you for taking the time to read my book. If you have enjoyed the content in this book and found it useful, please take a moment to subscribe to my mailing list at http://www.bit.ly/30MinuteSales where you will not only receive FREE BONUS content, but also be made aware of upcoming releases and discounts before they are made public.

Thanks again. Please take a moment and review this book on Amazon as well. Your feedback means a lot to me.

Review Here:
http://bit.ly/30MinuteReviews

www.ingramcontent.com/pod-product-compliance
Lightning Source LLC
Chambersburg PA
CBHW021008180526
45163CB00005B/1933